# CONTENTS

Stories by Maureen Spurgeon

First published 1998
by Brown Watson, England

Reprinted 2001, 2003, 2005, 2007,
2010, 2011, 2013, 2015, 2016, 2017,
2018 (twice), 2019, 2020, 2021

ISBN: 978-0-7097-1257-2
© 1998 Brown Watson, England
Printed in Malaysia

# *Christmas*
## *Stories*

## Book 3

**Brown Watson**

ENGLAND

# THE NIGHT BEFORE CHRISTMAS

**'A Visit from St. Nicholas'**
**by Clement C. Moore**

*Illustrated by Colin Petty*

'Twas the night before Christmas,

when all through the house

Not a creature was stirring,

not even a mouse;

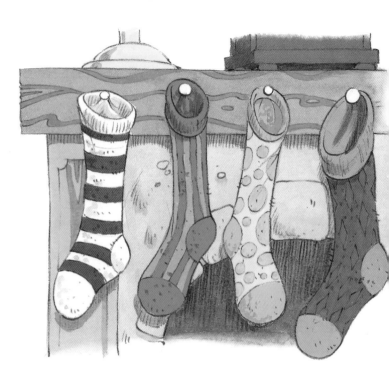

The stockings were hung
by the chimney with care,
In hopes that St. Nicholas
soon would be there.

The children were nestled
all snug in their beds,
While visions of sugarplums
danced in their heads;

And mamma in her kerchief,

and I in my cap,

Had just settled our brains

for a long winter nap;

When out on the lawn

there arose such a clatter,

I sprang from my bed

to see what was the matter.

Away to the window
I flew like a flash,
Tore open the shutters
and threw up the sash.

The moon, on the breast
of the new-fallen snow,
Gave a lustre of midday
to objects below,

When, what to my wondering
eyes should appear,
But a miniature sleigh
and eight tiny reindeer,

With a little old driver

so lively and quick,

I knew in a moment

it must be St. Nick.

More rapid than eagles,

 his coursers they came,

And he whistled and shouted

 and called them by name:

"Now, Dasher! Now, Dancer!

Now, Prancer and Vixen!

On Comet! On Cupid!
On Donner and Blitzen!
To the top of the porch,
to the top of the wall,

Now, dash away! Dash away!

Dash away all!"

As dry leaves that before

the wild hurricane fly,

When they meet with an obstacle,

mount to the sky,

So up to the housetop
the coursers they flew,
With the sleigh full of toys,
and St. Nicholas, too.

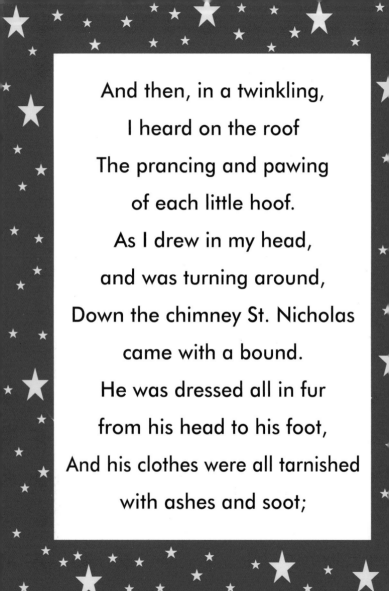

And then, in a twinkling,

I heard on the roof

The prancing and pawing

of each little hoof.

As I drew in my head,

and was turning around,

Down the chimney St. Nicholas

came with a bound.

He was dressed all in fur

from his head to his foot,

And his clothes were all tarnished

with ashes and soot;

A bundle of toys

    he had flung on his back,

And he looked like a pedlar

    just opening his pack.

His eyes – how they twinkled!

    His dimples – how merry!

His cheeks were like roses,

    his nose like a cherry.

His droll little mouth

was drawn up like a bow,

And the beard on his chin

was as white as the snow.

He had a broad face
and a little round belly
That shook when he laughed
like a bowlful of jelly.

28

He was chubby and plump,
a right jolly old elf,
And I laughed when I saw him
in spite of myself.

A wink of his eye

    and a twist of his head

Soon gave me to know

    I had nothing to dread.

He spoke not a word,

　　but went straight to his work,

And filled all the stockings;

　　then turned with a jerk,

And laying his finger

aside of his nose,

And giving a nod,

up the chimney he rose.

He sprang to his sleigh,
   to his team gave a whistle
And away they all flew
   like the down of a thistle.

But I heard him exclaim,

'ere he drove out of sight,

"Happy Christmas to all,

and to all a good night!"

# THE
# CHRISTMAS
# FAIRY

*Illustrated by Colin Petty*

Two men were talking outside in the street. Dolly could hear them quite clearly from the window sill where she sat.

"Quite a nip in the air," said one. "Sure sign of Christmas on the way," said the other. "We always look forward to Christmas in our house!"

Dolly shivered, wishing she could pull her thin dress closer around her. If only she were still at the big house, she thought! Christmas had always been special, there...

That was when Dolly had lived in a big dolls' house, with the most delicious, warm smells wafting up from the downstairs kitchen and decorations in every room!

Once, there had even been a
Christmas tree in the big nursery.
There was a fairy doll at the very
top, smiling down at them all.
Dolly thought she was beautiful.

"If only," she thought, "if only I could wear a lovely dress like that, and hold a wand in my hand... What wishes I'd give everyone for Christmas!"

Years passed, and the little girl who owned Dolly grew up. But, somehow, Dolly was always there at Christmas. Young visitors who called often played with her.

Dolly loved every minute – until, one Christmas, she got quite a shock. "Look, Mummy!" called out one little girl. "Look at this funny, old doll!"

"It was my mother's when she was about your age," smiled her aunty. "Then she gave her to me. When I have a little girl, I expect I'll pass it on to her, too!"

There had been many little girls over the years, Dolly remembered. They all grew up – but she stayed the same. And Christmas was still her favourite time of the year.

Then, one Christmas, something happened. Underneath the big Christmas tree, there was a big parcel tied with ribbon. The little girl could hardly wait to open it!

Inside was quite the most splendid doll. She had soft curly hair, big blue eyes which opened and closed, and the loveliest dress Dolly had ever seen.

"I shall call her Arabella!" cried the little girl in delight. "Look, Mummy and Daddy! She can walk, too!"

Dolly could not help feeling sad.

The little girl played with Arabella
every day after that.
By the end of the Christmas
holidays, Dolly knew she had
been forgotten.

"What are you going to do with that old wooden doll, dear?" the little girl's Daddy asked his wife. "Is there anyone we know who would like it?"

"Not really," answered the little girl's Mummy. "Besides, children don't play with wooden dolls nowadays. She can go on the window sill for now."

And except for the times when the windows were cleaned or the window sill dusted, Dolly was quite alone. As Christmas drew near, she felt so cold, so miserable.

"Nobody would miss me here," she thought, looking out into the street. It was terrible, hearing the two men sounding so cheerful when she had never been so unhappy.

Suddenly, the door opened and the little girl's mother hurried across the room to open the window.

"Are you collecting rubbish?" she called to the two men.

"Can you take a pile of old newspapers?"
"Be right with you, ma'am!" one shouted back. They didn't see Dolly falling out into the street!

She lay there for what seemed a very long time, cold and wet and wishing she could cry for help.
Every so often, she would hear somebody talking about Christmas.

"Hello!" cried a voice, and Dolly
felt a rough hand picking her up.
"What have we got here?"
"Something for the rubbish tip, I
reckon, Mike!" said someone else.

Fear made Dolly feel colder than ever. Then the first man said, "Oh, I might as well take her home. Maybe my little girl will like her." Dolly did hope so!

"Well," said the man when he showed Dolly to his daughter. "What do you think?"
"Why can't she move her arms and legs?" asked the little girl.

"Because she's made of wood, silly!" laughed the little girl's mother. "Your Nana had one just like this when I was about your age. She was fun to play with!"

"And," her mummy went on, "she's just what we need for Christmas!" Soon, the little girl was wiping all the mud and dirt off Dolly. And, as for her mummy...

She made Dolly a pretty fairy dress with silver wings, a tinsel crown and a lovely, silver wand. Dolly was ready to grant all the wishes made around the Christmas tree!

"I wonder if Dolly gets a wish, too?" said the little girl.
"You know," said her mummy, "I think she's had her wish already!"
"And so I have," thought Dolly.

# THE
# MAGIC
# REINDEER

*Illustrated by Stephen Holmes*

Ronnie the reindeer was always in trouble! "Oh, Ronnie!" cried Mother Deer. "How DID you get your antlers tangled up in this holly bush?"

"RONNIE!" roared Stag. "Why MUST you charge through the stream and splash water about? Look, I'm dripping wet!"

But as soon as Ronnie saw a bird in the sky or leaves rustling on a bush, off he'd dash. Then it would be, "Ronnie! Don't tread in our water!" or "Ronnie! You've splashed us with mud!"

All this made Ronnie feel very sad. If only he could do something really special, he thought, something to make all the other reindeer really proud of him...

Ronnie tried hard to think what he could do. But long after the other reindeer were asleep and night had fallen, he still hadn't thought of anything. He gave a big sigh, looking up at the sky.

Father Christmas was out on a practice sleigh-ride, ready for Christmas Eve. But Ronnie didn't know that. He was watching the reindeer flying! If they could fly, he told himself, he could, too!

Ronnie began practising the very next day. Off he went to the top of a hill. He took a deep breath, ran as fast as he could, then jumped, flapping his hooves about and hoping he would fly!

But flying wasn't nearly so easy as it looked! Ronnie just fell to the ground, squashing a clump of lovely, fresh grass! "Ronnie!" roared Stag. "You're getting into trouble AGAIN!"

Ronnie tried all sorts of things –
hopping about on each hoof,
jumping up and down... being
so busy and moving about so
much, he hardly noticed the
snow which had begun to fall...

And this time, before Ronnie could make a jump, his back hooves slid on the icy ground. Up he went into the air, his legs moving all at once. Ronnie could hardly believe it!

When Ronnie landed in the soft snow, he could see that he was quite a long way from where he had jumped - and that could only mean one thing! "I CAN fly!" he cried. "I can FLY!"

It was so exciting, Ronnie didn't want to stop! Again and again, he tried sliding on the snow, then lifting up his hooves and sailing through the air! "Look at me!" he cried. "I'm FLYING!"

Some of the other reindeer had
already seen him! Off they went
to tell Stag and Mother Deer
about Ronnie learning to fly!
But someone else had seen
Ronnie, too...

"Oh, no!" groaned Father Christmas. "That little reindeer down there is trying to fly! And I thought EVERYONE knew that only MY reindeer can fly across the sky!"

Just then, Ronnie took another jump, flapped his legs and his hooves about, and fell down — THUMP!

Poor Ronnie! He could not help grinding his teeth in pain!

"I must do something about this," Father Christmas decided. "Steady, my reindeer. Let me get a sprinkle of stardust!" Soon, he knew, Ronnie would try to fly yet again.

Sure enough, the little reindeer ran over the snow. Then he lifted his legs, tucked in his hooves, and... WHOOSH! Up he flew into the sky in a shower of magic stardust!

84

With stars twinkling and the moon shining, Ronnie could see all the trees and bushes, now far, far below. A cool wind blew on his hooves and his legs until they didn't hurt at all.

"Oh," said Ronnie, "now I know how it REALLY feels to fly!"
"You had worked hard, trying to learn," said Father Christmas. "You deserved to have your Christmas wish come true."

By now, the other reindeer had called Stag and Mother Deer.
"Ronnie? Flying?" roared Stag.
"Rubbish! Where is he?"
"If he's got into trouble," said Mother Deer, "I'll —"

But none of them ever knew what she would do. Because, at that moment, the moon came out from behind a cloud, making all the deer look up into the starry sky.

"It's Father Christmas!" breathed the little reindeer.

"And his reindeer sleigh..." added Stag, almost in a whisper.

"And RONNIE!" cried Mother Deer. "He really CAN fly!"

Father Christmas guided his sleigh behind a mass of white, snowy cloud.

"Time for you to go, Ronnie!" he smiled. "This moonbeam will take you safely home."

Sliding down a moonbeam was as much fun as flying. "Thank you, Father Christmas!" cried Ronnie. "I hope I see you again!" "You will, Ronnie!" laughed Father Christmas. "You will!"

Ronnie landed safely on all four hooves. Now Stag, Mother Deer and all the reindeer wanted to hear about how he had flown with Father Christmas across the starry skies!

And if he slid on the snow, or fell in the mud or trod in the water, nobody minded too much. They were all so proud to know such a clever, wonderful, splendid reindeer like Ronnie!

## Stories I have read

Christmas on the Farm ☐

Santa's Little Helper ☐

The Christmas Fairy ☐

The Night Before Christmas ☐

Santa's Busy Day ☐